D0938361

The Perfect Ofsted Lesson

Wow. What a book! Normally I put educational reading at the bottom of my to-do list but this held my attention from the front through to the back. I loved the way it was set out in steps, with very useful strategies at each step. The strategies are varied and do work. It has quality educational research behind it but is written in a very accessible style. It is a must for every teacher.

The title is such a winner and the content really does deliver what it says on the cover.

Glen Alexander, Deputy Head teacher,
Archbishop Ilsley Catholic Technology College

I found this book to be a super read with practical advice and strategies which all teachers regardless of where they are in their career can use in their next lesson.
Jackie demystifies what makes that elusive outstanding lesson for Ofsted into a really positive experience for both students and teachers.
We will certainly be using it as a resource to further develop learning and teaching in our school.

Ranjit Samra, Head of Southam College

A concise practical approach to delivering the perfect Ofsted lesson – the book builds upon the key characteristics of an outstanding lesson giving practical ideas of how it can be achieved and more importantly how this can be demonstrated in a short time to Ofsted inspectors. The format is clear and accessible and gives useful points for debate and discussion amongst teachers. This book is for all teachers whether new to teaching or an experienced practitioner – it acts as an aide memoire for all to reflect on their practice.

Julie Summerfield, Headteacher of Horndean School

The Perfect Ofsted Lesson picks up all the key Ofsted related points as regards an outstanding lesson. Jackie emphasises right from the off the most important point – it's about the learning! All the other key points are then covered very systematically – the engagement of students, high expectations, higher order questioning, use of assessment to support learning and using resources such as LSAs and lots more. Running through the text is the constant reminder that this can't be pulled out of a hat – it's a process and teachers need to develop and train their students to work in this way.

Gulshan Kayembe, Education Consultant
and experienced school inspector

THE PERFECT
LESSON

Ofsted

Jackie Beere Edited by Ian Gilbert

Crown House Publishing Limited
www.crownhouse.co.uk – www.crownhousepublishing.com

First published by

Crown House Publishing Ltd
Crown Buildings, Bancyfelin, Carmarthen, Wales, SA33 5ND, UK
www.crownhouse.co.uk

and

Crown House Publishing Company LLC
6 Trowbridge Drive, Suite 5, Bethel, CT 06801, USA
www.crownhousepublishing.com

First published 2010. Reprinted 2011 (twice).

British Library Cataloguing-in-Publication Data
A catalogue entry for this book is available
from the British Library.

ISBN 978-184590460-9

LCCN 2010937331

Printed and bound in the UK by
Gomer Press, Llandysul, Ceredigion

This book is dedicated to all the teachers in the world who are making such an amazing difference to so many children. I have the privilege of working with them and seeing their dedication and determination. They are creating our future.

Contents

Foreword

Nobody quite knows where the phrase 'tail wagging the dog' comes from but, like cowboys and denim jeans, it probably originated in America in the mid-19th century.

We do, however, know where Ofsted comes from (the Education and Inspections Act of 2006) although, these days, we have less notice of when they will be coming.

In the early days, the school inspection seemed to be all about bashing teachers and making schools feel bad, with Chris Woodhead leading the charge like a latter-day witch-finder general. These days a more enlightened approach does genuinely seem to indicate that Ofsted is on the lookout for good practice and inspectors, good ones at least, seem to do their best to celebrate good learning (as opposed to teaching) when and if it happens.

And it is this distinction – that an outstanding lesson isn't marked by what the teacher teaches but what the learner learns – that is at the heart of this new book from the prolific pen of Jackie Beere.

Jackie's educational career from supply teacher to AST to headteacher to educational advisor to governments, School Improvement Partner, author and speaker (via Buckingham Palace to pick up her OBE for services to education) means that she is well placed to cut through all the double-speak and waffle when it comes to what makes schools tick. What's more, when it comes to teaching and learning, her experience and pioneering work on skills-based learning and what is known as the Competency Curriculum, mean that she knows exactly what constitutes the sort of good practice that Ofsted is looking for these days.

Which brings us to dogs and their tails. It might seem to be the wrong way round, planning lessons that will tick the boxes of a hypothetical inspector who may or not appear in your classroom at some point in the next four years and, even just a short while ago, I would have agreed. But these days a 'good', 'outstanding' or indeed 'perfect' Ofsted lesson bears all the hallmarks of the sort of practice that Jackie Beere and the rest of us at Independent Thinking have been banging on about for years – a focus on learning, the development of thinking skills, opportunities for independent learning, a variety of strategies that take into account different elements of the individual learner's preferences, strengths and weaknesses, the use of positive emotions, great relationships, clear goals, metacognition, creativity and the willingness to take a risk or two, you name it, it's all there. And this book tells you just how to use such strategies and employ them in way that is clear and practical and will – and we know this because we have asked them – tick all of Ofsted's boxes.

One last thing – as Jackie is at pains to point out, don't wait until the actual envelope arrives on your proverbial doormat before you start to implement the many strategies outlined in this book. Make them part of your day-to-day teaching now and the more you practise them the less stressful the day of that fateful visit will be. In fact, it won't be so much an inspection as the opportunity to show off just how good the teaching and learning really is in your classroom.

In fact, not so much tail wagging the dog as best in class.

Ian Gilbert
Suffolk
October 2010

Acknowledgements

One day my daughter Carrie asked me to do a workshop at a conference she was producing called 'Facilitating the Perfect Ofsted Lesson'. She couldn't find anyone else who would do it so, of course, I stepped in. I planned a session based on the latest Ofsted criteria that really focused on how to demonstrate progress in learning. I then tried out my idea on my other daughter, who is a teacher in a challenging school experiencing constant lesson observations. Lucy used this technique with great success. In fact the inspector said, 'You really nailed the progress in learning.' I want to thank my two daughters for their inspiration, love and support.

I also want to thank the team at Crown House Publishing, my husband John who has spent many hours checking the book for me and Ian Gilbert who has worked his magic with encouraging and helpful feedback.

Introduction

Most of the very best teachers have experienced an unsatisfactory judgement at some time in their careers. Learn from it, and it will work as a positive force in your development. Dwell on it, beat yourself up about it, argue about it, and it could be destructive and very demoralising.

Remember, an observation is only a snapshot of your teaching

The aim of this book is to make that snapshot look not only outstanding but for it to truly reflect your everyday outstanding teaching.

We all want to do well and impress observers in our lessons. This book is written to help you achieve the very best results you can when an official observer or inspector pays a call. However, the guidance will also help you to develop your teaching techniques and become the great career teacher you want to be.

The advice is not a prescriptive set of rules but suggests a model around which you can build your own ideas. Its purpose is to help you deliver a lesson that will demonstrate to any observer that the students in your class are making great progress in their learning under your supervision. 'Progress' is the magic ingredient required for 'outstanding' lessons.

The advice is easy to apply – no matter what subject you teach or what sort of teacher you are. Many different teachers have successfully implemented the strategies offered here and adapted them to suit their different styles, personalities and classes.

The book begins by offering seven simple steps towards creating the 'perfect' lesson. The following chapters then elaborate on these steps, explaining the key ideas within them in more detail. You can read these straightaway or look them up at a later date if needed.

You don't need the 'wow' factor to deliver an excellent lesson but you do need engaged, enthusiastic and determined students who are driven to make progress because they want to learn. You need to be able to nurture this ethos through having very high expectations for all of your students and by using your expertise to enthuse them about new learning.

You also need to be able to accurately measure and respond to the progress they make in your lesson in order to plan the next phase. Your classes have to make a contribution to the value-added results of your school. Therefore your students need to make progress in their lessons. They must move forward with their learning – and *know* they have. And know how they did it – so that they can do it again next time. Equally, if they haven't made enough progress, they need to know why and how to fix it.

Introduction

In my experience, students and teachers who understand the theory of 'learning to learn' and have nurtured the habits of PLTs (Personal, Learning and Thinking skills) find it is far easier to achieve success. This is because such an understanding requires developing a language with which to discuss and reflect on learning and how it works. With the right vocabulary, students and teachers can talk about how learning has worked and, perhaps more importantly, how it has stalled or floundered and what they have learned from that outcome.

An observer or inspector needs to see a learning environment that is challenging learners to exceed beyond their expectations and feel the tangible excitement of brains making connections to new learning. This will only develop and be evident to observers if the advice offered in this book becomes part of your everyday practice and is demonstrated in the students' books and class discussions and in the classroom dynamics, all of which take time to develop. You will know when you get this right because you will actually wish every day for someone official to walk through the door and see the fantastic learning going on in your classroom!

'When observing lessons, a connection should be made to the impact that teaching and the use of assessment have on learners' behaviour, progress and the *quality of learning*, making specific reference to *different groups of learners*.'

Ofsted (2010)

Chapter 1

The perfect lesson in simple stages: meeting the new criteria and delivering progress in learning

Step 1. Know what they are looking for

How can you make sure that in the brief time an inspector (or other observer) is in your classroom that your lesson ticks enough boxes to impress – and gains that 'outstanding' grade?

Sharing the criteria for success is essential for any learning experience. If you (or your students) do not know what they are expected to strive for, how do you (or they) know they have achieved success? So, with this in mind, the Ofsted 2010 grade descriptors for an outstanding lesson are shown overleaf.

The quality of pupils' learning and their progress*

The pupils acquire knowledge, develop understanding and learn and practise skills exceptionally well.

Pupils demonstrate excellent concentration and are rarely off task, even in extended periods without direction from an adult.

Pupils have developed resilience when tackling challenging activities in a range of subjects.

Pupils' keenness and commitment to succeed in all aspects of school life and their ability to grasp opportunities to extend and improve their learning are exceptional.

Progress is at least good in each key stage, key subjects and for different groups, and is exemplary in some.

The quality of teaching and the use of assessment to support learning*

Teaching is at least good and much is outstanding, with the result that the pupils are making exceptional progress.

It is highly effective in inspiring pupils and ensuring that they learn extremely well.

Excellent subject knowledge is applied consistently to challenge and inspire pupils.

Resources, including new technology, make a marked contribution to the quality of learning, as does the precisely targeted support provided by other adults.

Teachers and other adults are acutely aware of their pupils' capabilities and of their prior learning and understanding, and plan very effectively to build on these.

Marking and dialogue between teachers, other adults and pupils are consistently of a very high quality.

Pupils understand in detail how to improve their work and are consistently supported in doing so.

Teachers systematically and effectively check pupils' understanding throughout lessons, anticipating where they may need to intervene and doing so with striking impact on the quality of learning

* Source: Ofsted 2010.

Note: Grade descriptors for 'good', 'satisfactory' and 'inadequate' can be found by typing 'The evaluation schedule for schools' into a search engine. The *really* keen may also want to look at some of the other descriptors in the sections on 'outcomes' and 'how effective is the provision?', as well as others that have a bearing on the classroom such as 'behaviour'.

Searching for the 'x' factor: what are the magic ingredients that will make your lesson outstanding?

The first sentences in the previous table identify the key ingredients for success:

▓ The pupils acquire knowledge, develop understanding and learn and practise skills *exceptionally well*.

▓ Teaching is at least good and much is outstanding, with the result that the pupils are making *exceptional progress*.

In summary, therefore, the 'x' factor means demonstrating *exceptional progress in learning* in your lesson.

The following are some of the other essential ingredients required for an outstanding lesson:

▓ Demonstrating expert subject knowledge and skills.

▓ Demonstrating that you can communicate effectively.

▓ Differentiating for various groups of learners.

▓ Engaging and motivating students.

- Developing independent and resilient learners.
- Delivering skills and content essential for passing exams.
- Assessment as part of developing progress in learning.
- Challenging the most able learners.
- Using technology and teaching assistants to make an impact on learning.
- Effective collaborative learning and peer review.
- Effective classroom management.
- Sharing the criteria for success.

So how can you make sure that you demonstrate the above when being observed or inspected? Practice! It may take you a while, but getting it wrong and learning to get it right *before* you are observed will pay huge dividends for that lesson when the inspector does walk through the door. The following chapters will give you much more detail on how to do this. However, first consider the remaining steps towards the 'perfect' lesson and then dip in to the other chapters as you need them.

> Tell the students beforehand that an observer may come in and may wish to talk to them – then they will be on your side.

Step 2. Be present and in control, right from the start

Set up the learning environment

> The relationships you have with your students are the most important aspect of setting up your learning environment.

Students should expect to start work as soon as they come into the classroom without you directing them. This strategy should cover the time it takes for all the students to arrive. It neatly shows how you are completely and effortlessly in control and makes a great impression on that extra (Ofsted) visitor.

Get the students into the habit of self-starting in every lesson by setting little challenges, questions or tasks on the board that they *know* they are expected to get on with. These can be anagrams, puzzles, true or false statements, recaps of the previous lesson(s), unexpected questions for debate, music challenges and so on. Reward effort for these tasks as part of your reward-and-sanction classroom policy.

It is a good idea to have music on as students come in and are getting on with these tasks (see Nina Jackson's *The Little Book of Music in the Classroom* for some suggestions). Then, when you switch the music off, the students know it is time for the lesson proper to start.

While the students are completing the tasks, circulate, smile, greet them individually by name and make them feel welcome. You could get the students to assess each other's work if appropriate.

This will mean that you can start the main part of the lesson when *you* are ready and useful work is already taking place.

Step 3. The starter

A starter should stimulate curiosity and open-mindedness and prepare the brain for learning. These can be random or linked to the subject.

> Engaging the emotional brain makes
> your class curious and attentive.

A starter can be a Thunk, a curiosity or a challenge of some sort.

A Thunk

This is a question (from Ian Gilbert's *The Little Book of Thunks*) that has no right or wrong answer but which makes you think. This prepares students to be open-minded and consider various options. For example:

- If you always got what you wished for would you always be happy?
- Can you point to where the sky begins?
- What has the most freedom – an ant or a school child?
- Is a person who has a face transplant still the same person?
- Which is heavier, an inflated or deflated balloon?

Students can think of the next question or make up their own Thunks as part of the starter.

A curiosity

For example:

- A box – students have to guess what the contents are.
- A wig or hat – someone can try it on and guess the character it belongs to.
- A message in a bottle – students have to guess the message and who sent it.

Chapter 1

A creative challenge in pairs

For example:

- What was the first pop song you ever heard and the one you heard most recently?
- What were the three most popular babies' names in 1999 and which three will be most popular in 2020?
- Guess the most common and least common food that everyone in the class had for breakfast.

Work for, party with or send to the jungle

A fun task that helps students understand personal preferences. Which would you do with the following famous names and why?

For example:

- Prince William, John Terry, Russell Brand
- Cheryl Cole, Davina McCall, Fern Britton
- Nick Clegg, Gordon Brown, David Cameron

> Be energetic and enthusiastic.
> Channel any nerves into passion!

Room 101

This is the room full of your worst nightmare. For Winston in George Orwell's *1984* it was rats. What three things would you put in Room 101 and why?

The starter tasks can also link explicitly to one of the Personal, Learning and Thinking skills (PLTs). Success could earn points that accumulate over time and gain rewards. Some examples of tasks involving the PLTs appear in the table opposite.

Personal, Learning and Thinking skills	Task
Self-manager	Draw a face that depicts the different moods you have experienced today so far
Effective participator	Write down five things you will do in this lesson to help others learn
Creative thinker	Design a logo and slogan for this subject/lesson
Reflective learner	Create a mind map of what we did last lesson
Independent enquirer	Write three questions you need to ask about what we did last lesson
Teamworker	Think of three promises you will make to your team to help it work well

Step 4. Set objectives or learning outcomes: engage them in the learning

Describe simply and *exactly* what you want the students to be able to do by the end of the lesson. Do this at two levels (at least) for differentiation.

> Setting high expectations is the single most important thing you can do to ensure good progress in learning. Make sure specific groups of students are aware of what they need to do to make progress.

This is the crucial moment when you engage the students in the exciting task ahead and explain that it will make a difference to them personally. To succeed you must communicate your expectation of success and your personal excitement about the subject – what they can achieve and why it is important. Ensure that students with particular needs (the most able, the least able, particular ethnic minorities, girls, boys or vulnerable students) have that extra bit of attention, resources or scaffolding to ensure that they know how to make progress.

Doing this effectively shows that you *'and other adults are acutely aware of their pupils' capabilities and of their prior learning and understanding, and plan very effectively to build on these'* (Ofsted 2010).

Setting up learning outcomes that connect
with students and their world are crucial to a
successful lesson.

How can you convince the students that learning is a journey
and that they have an amazing capacity to progress during
this lesson? There are three steps to doing this:

1. Explaining (with passion) what success in achieving the
   objectives will look like and feel like (i.e. the 'brilliant
   outcome').

2. Showing them that achieving the objectives is part of a
   learning journey towards a greater goal by using a
   continuum line (see diagram on page 19).

3. By setting one or more personal skills objectives for
   individual (or targeted) students (see the boxes in the
   diagrams on page 19).

Draw a continuum line that leads to the 'brilliant outcome' they are heading towards in their learning journey. At the start of the activity students should decide where they are along the line. After the task they then mark where they are now to demonstrate what (if any) progress they have made in the lesson towards the outcome. The same can be done for the PLTs which will help the students towards self-assessment of particular skills. These are just as crucial for an outstanding lesson.

> We need to ensure that our students develop deep, lasting learning and a set of life skills that will more effectively equip them for the real world.

See the following example:

Objective/learning outcomes	Long-term personal goal
By the end of this lesson you will be able to:	
1. Note how the writer has used language effectively (Level 4)	I will read and understand great writing so that I can learn to write brilliantly myself
2. Comment on how the writer uses language to engage the reader using quotations (Level 5)	
PLTs (teamworker): Show how well you work with others	I make a big difference to my team's performance through listening, working together and setting high standards
PLTs (independent enquirer): Work independently and find things out for myself	I can think about what I need to do to succeed in a task and do it really well on my own

A huge arrow across your classroom wall will enable you to talk to the whole class about how they have progressed in the lesson. By using sticky notes you can show their progress along their learning journey.

Step 5. The main lesson activity/activities

This is where the teacher's input really comes in to facilitate the learning.

'Pupils demonstrate excellent concentration and are rarely off task, even in extended periods without direction from an adult. Excellent subject knowledge is used to challenge and inspire pupils.'

Ofsted (2010)

In your classroom there needs to be:

1. A challenging level of subject knowledge – a passion for the subject and an ability to communicate it in ways that enthuse the students

2. Active, collaborative learning – it is crucial to show students are able to work, on task, without adult supervision.

3. A choice of challenging activities or approaches available.

4. Lots of higher order questions (which you don't answer for them).

5. Visual aids and practical activities.

The first three points, **challenge**, **collaboration** and **choice**, must be present to deliver an outstanding lesson because:

- **Challenge** is the way to ensure that expectations are high and learners are working to *make progress* in their learning.
- **Collaboration** ensures that students work together, independently of the teacher, to achieve the 'brilliant outcomes'.
- **Choice** engages the learners and makes them feel committed to the task.

Good collaborative activities can help to connect the learning with the world at home. But, most importantly, they let the *students* lead the lesson. They give the students a chance to talk more than the teacher and they tap into the natural talents in the room. The teacher should not always be the 'sage on the stage'.

Collaborative activities also allow the teacher to be a much better facilitator of learning. They let the students show the following from the (Ofsted 2010) descriptor for 'outstanding' learning:

- 'excellent concentration';
- that they 'are rarely off task without direction from an adult';
- 'resilience when tackling challenging activities';
- 'keenness and commitment to succeed'.

If you dominate the lesson, when are the students going to show these qualities?

In addition, collaborative activities can be highly effective in inspiring pupils and ensuring that they learn extremely well. When you work with small groups they help you to hit many more of the 'outstanding' grade descriptors for quality of teaching by enabling you to (Ofsted 2010):

- use your 'excellent subject knowledge ... to challenge and inspire pupils';
- promote that very high quality 'marking and dialogue between teachers, other adults and pupils';
- show that you are checking that 'pupils understand in detail how to improve their work and are consistently supported in doing so';
- show that you 'systematically and effectively check pupils' understanding throughout lessons, anticipating where they may need to intervene and doing so with striking impact on the quality of learning'.

> Managing great teamwork that helps
> learning progress is a key skill for achieving a high
> grade in an observation.

You can also set up group work or teamwork that develops employability or personal skills (i.e. the PLTs). But before doing this, coach students in the four stages of group work: forming, storming, norming and performing (Tuckman 1965). Roles within groups and the skills needed for effective leadership also need to be taught.

> Stand back and support students' abilities to
> resolve conflict in group work.

Differentiation means setting different learning outcomes for different groups of students so they are all challenged to make good progress. When you set your outcomes make sure you describe the success criteria for different ability groups (even in streamed classes you will have a range of abilities). For example:

For a Level 3 you will be able to ....

For a Level 4 you will be able to ....

For a Level 5 you will be able to ....

Three useful beliefs which underpin outstanding teaching:

1. We always underestimate the capabilities of young people.

2. Every child wants to succeed.

3. We get what we expect.

Collaborative projects are group challenges that involve choosing tasks around a cross-curricular or single subject theme and completing them by negotiation. The end product will be demonstrated to the whole class and celebrated as part of the assessment.

Assessment for such projects can be subject based or skills based and this will depend on the learning outcomes that have been set and monitored by both teachers and students. There are two examples of collaborative projects below and more are available in *The Competency Curriculum Toolkit* by Jackie Beere and Helen Boyle.

Choice engages the emotional brain and enhances motivation for students.

Note that these examples all have an element of *choice* in the tasks and an onus on completing the work as a team. The outcomes should be presented by the group and, as far as is possible, quality control should be given to the team.

In outstanding schools, Ofsted (2009) said that:

Consistency of approach is a characteristic shared by all 12 schools. They are truly corporate cultures, with staff and usually students working for each other sensitively and cooperatively. Students do not receive mixed messages or perceive staff to have vastly different values. They see common purpose: adults who are working in students' interests, who like being in the school, who care for it and are ambitious for its future.

An element of competition can be added by allocating points for different tasks, the diagrams next two pages are a good example of this. The activities shown on page 26 are compulsory and an additional two activities should be chosen from page 27.

Research Newton's Third Law of Motion.
5 points

Research Newton's First Law of Motion.
5 points

Research Newton's Second Law of Motion.
5 points

Build a water rocket.
10 points

Water Rocket Project

Compulsory activities.

Launch your rocket and measure the distance it travelled.
3 points

Write a detailed evaluation of the performance of your rocket.
5 points

What is PSI? Why is it important in launching a rocket?
5 points

Draw diagrams of your water rocket showing the forces acting on it at different times.
2 points

Present your project as a poem or rap.
2 points

Present a piece of drama work to illustrate Newton's Laws of Motion.
7 points

Water Rocket Project

Choose 2 other activities to complete.

Brainstorm for ideas on how to improve the performance of a water rocket.
2 points

Compare the performance of your rocket with that of another group.
2 points

Shoot a video of your rocket in flight.
2 points

Present your project as a news article.
5 points

Here is another example, this time points are not necessary.

Subject and skills links: English, Food, History, ICT, Creative Thinking, Teamworking.

Agree as a group the murder story for your party.

Create a menu for the meal.

Research at least 4 historical figures to invite to your party.

Murder Mystery Dinner Party

Design the invitations. Include a mystery riddle (optional).

Write the script for each guest to introduce themselves.

Design or describe the costumes for the guests.

Design your own tasks for the team.

See www.jackiebeere.com for more examples of collaborative projects

Step 6. Dish up the DIRT ... often!

DIRT = Dedicated Improvement and Reflection Time through assessment as learning

The process of learning is a journey. It is essential to raise awareness of this by frequently reminding students to check their learning processes and progress. (What have you learned? How have you learned it? How far have you travelled towards the learning outcome?) There should be regular checkpoints in the lesson that become part of the assessment *as* learning process. A very important part of this is the teacher's awareness of how different groups of students have performed and what their next steps should be (another good reason to do collaborative learning and not simply to lead from the front). Pay particular attention to the most able, special educational needs students, girls, boys, ethnic minorities and children in care, as appropriate. You need to know who these students are and how they have progressed. They need to know too!

Inspectors may take into account the extent to which:

- teachers and adults ensure that pupils know how well they are doing and are provided with clear detailed steps for improvement
- effective questioning is used to gauge pupils' understanding and reshape explanations and tasks where this is needed
- teachers and adults assess pupils' progress accurately and are alert to pupils' lack of understanding during the lesson so that they can move swiftly to put it right.

Ofsted (2010)

With DIRT you can help ensure that (Ofsted 2010):

- 'pupils understand in detail how to improve their work and are consistently supported in doing so';
- you 'systematically and effectively check pupils' understanding throughout lessons, anticipating where they may need to intervene and doing so with striking impact on the quality of learning'.

Reviewing and reflecting

> Ideally, students must be self-motivated, resilient and driven to make progress in their own learning.

This is the quality control moment when students work on their own or together to improve their work.

When students know what the success criteria are then they are better able to gauge their progress. But they need to focus on the quality of the work produced too. A checklist that relates to success criteria is helpful here. You could use Assessment of Pupil Progress (APP) student worksheets to enable students to begin to self- or peer-assess the work they produce.

Working to redraft, improve and amend against success criteria and acting on constructive criticism is a vital part of the learning journey. It also gives the students more control over – and responsibility for – the outcomes. It also prevents marking from being a mysterious process that only goes on in the teacher's head.

> High quality self-assessment and peer-assessment gives learners the ability to discuss and develop their own progress.

An example of success criteria from an English lesson is shown below.

WRITING	**Level 3** **In most writing**
AF1 Write imaginative, interesting and thoughtful texts	▪ include relevant ideas ▪ try to add to basic information ▪ try to show a viewpoint even if I don't all the time
AF2 Produce texts which are appropriate to purpose, audience and style	▪ try to show the purpose ▪ try to use some features and the right style

Level 4 Across a range of writing	Level 5 Across a range of writing
�či choose relevant ideas ▓ develop some ideas in detail and description while showing a clear viewpoint	▓ develop relevant ideas with some imagination ▓ develop ideas suited to the form of writing ▓ establish a consistent viewpoint
▓ make the main purpose of my writing clear ▓ use appropriate features ▓ try to use the right style	▓ maintain the purpose of my writing ▓ show some features and the right style ▓ adapt some features when I need to

Step 7. Final plenary/review

The moment of truth: how far did we get towards our objectives?

At the end of the lesson a memorable plenary will sum up the learning outcomes. *If they haven't all made progress don't be afraid to acknowledge it.* This gives you a chance to explain what your next steps will be to ensure *all* students have learned what they need to know.

> Helping students to develop a language they can use to talk about their learning and how much progress they have made is an essential part of making assessment contribute to the process of learning.

Useful plenary techniques include:

- Having a huge learning progress arrow on the wall. Students pin their names on it to show how far they have progressed towards the learning outcome.
- Sticky notes for students to record three things they have learned – these can be placed on the door on the way out or shared in groups and prioritised.
- Mini-whiteboards and pens for writing down and showing key points from the lesson.

- Showing 5, 4, 3, 2, 1 fingers to indicate learning progress – 5 fingers means 'I really got it', 4 means 'I mostly got it', 3 means 'I got some of it' and so on.
- Students sit in a hotseat and make three points as a key character who would be an expert in the lesson outcome. They hand on to another class member who has to make two points, then down to one.
- Students write down the key learning points from the lesson on a piece of paper, fold them up and put them in a bag or box. Open it up next lesson and share the comments.
- Summarise the key learning in a headline. It is useful to have some mock-up newspapers made with blank headlines.

Always finish on time so that you don't miss out the final plenary.

The final plenary

Cut short other activities if necessary but make sure you have this chance to demonstrate the progress in learning and also make your own assessment about whether you have succeeded in achieving the learning outcome.

It should be very clear to any observer that students have made progress in learning and can demonstrate it. Where insufficient progress has been made it should be clear what the plan of action will be to address this next lesson. One of the most common criticisms is that teachers don't use assessment outcomes to inform future planning. Make it clear that you can see what each and every student has learned and what the next steps are to secure progress.

Finish the plenary by setting the scene for the next exciting learning experience that will build on the lesson.

> Our learners spend much of their time learning effectively at home – setting up their mobile phones, using social media and computer games. Make sure you link learning at school to learning at home – and cash in on their expertise!

Set homework or extended learning that connects with the progress made and links the learning to a wider context.

Top tip: Plenaries can take place throughout the lesson. Take a moment for a mini-plenary at any time in the session to gather evidence about the learning progress (especially if you have an observer or inspector with you). Moments taken to reflect on how the learning is progressing are an important part of an outstanding lesson.

Chapter 2

Preparing to be present in the classroom

I've learned that people will forget what you said, people will forget what you did, but people will never forget how you made them feel.

Maya Angelou

Preparing for the observer in your classroom: the mind–body connection

Your lesson is planned and you have your resources ready – including water to drink. Now start mentally rehearsing your lesson before you get there. This is an important part of your preparation. When you do the mental rehearsal, make sure that you are saying the phrases shown on page 45. Also, see yourself with positive body language – standing up in control of the class but relaxed and smiling. Breathe deeply, slowly and regularly.

Imagine yourself doing the following during the lesson: meet and greet the students. Look as if you are enjoying it and hear your voice – strong, loud and authoritative, full of warmth and sincerity. Calm the class, praise, explain the objectives and tasks. Move around the classroom with confidence. Hover around the students who may need extra focus and give them positive attention when they are on task. Make sure you take a moment to breathe and assess how well the lesson is going. Always keep good eye contact on a one-to-one level.

'Pupils' consistently thoughtful behaviour is an outstanding factor in their successful learning and creates an extremely positive school ethos.'

Ofsted (2010)

Regularly sweep the room to ensure you know *everything* that is going on – both in front of you and behind your back. This is very important, especially when you have an official observer. Get into the habit of having eyes in the back of your head in every lesson. Nothing is more powerful than giving the message that you know exactly what is happening in one corner of the room even when you are helping students in the opposite corner. When students are working collaboratively and in teams your role is to move around and support their learning, but keep half of your attention on the whole classroom environment to ensure a positive working atmosphere.

So, the rehearsal is over and you are now prepared, confident and ready to be observed.

This is what I was born for ...

Being present in the classroom means that you are 'in the moment' and all your energy and focus is there. Our attention can easily be hijacked by visitors, distracting behaviour from certain individuals, activity outside the room, our own problems, nervousness about the situation and so on. Ruthlessly attend to the teaching you are delivering and allow nothing to divert you from this. We have all experienced that moment when you become conscious of the sound of your own voice speaking and this can lead to anxiety sabotaging our performance. Just stay in the moment, focus your conscious attention on what you are saying and on the students in your classroom. Don't allow your mind to wander. This way you will perform at your best and maintain the authenticity essential for the lesson to work well.

Practise what you preach

Great teachers have a philosophy that says, 'Every mistake is a learning experience.' Make sure that you endorse this philosophy in your own working life. You will have bad lessons – lessons that go horribly wrong and make you feel like you should give up. If you are unlucky, these experiences may happen when someone is observing. If you put into practice the philosophy of learning from your mistakes, and make this a habit of your teaching, then you will always be able to adapt when a lesson goes wrong. Firstly, admit your mistakes – especially to the students. Get feedback from them as to why it didn't work and learn from this. Secondly, recognise when it has gone wrong and try something different. Thirdly, appreciate you can't know everything – sometimes they will know more than you (especially about mobile phones!). Exploit this and get them to share their expertise. Be confident that being a teacher doesn't mean you have to know everything – but you do know your subject and how to help kids learn. One of the most impressive aspects of the best lessons is seeing students take over and do some of the teaching.

> 'Pupils have a strong voice in decisions relating to their learning and wellbeing. The pupils' involvement in the school and their interaction in the wider community are substantial and highly valued.'
>
> Ofsted (2010)

Finally, if the lesson takes an unexpected turn – but this new direction will serve to extend their learning – don't simply stick to your plan (even if the inspector has a copy of it.) Explain that this is a great development and you are going to deviate a little to make the most of this new opportunity for learning. Make sure this isn't just a hobby horse of yours or of interest to only a small group of students. For example, one student may have a story that relates to the lesson; let them tell the story and then ask, 'What can we learn from this that fits with our learning outcome?'

Chapter 2

Behaviour management

Working hard on building the consistent classroom relationships described above is the key to managing behaviour.
Respect for each other and respect for the teacher should be
habitual behaviours that characterise your teaching. If the
lesson is interesting and expectations are high, behaviour
management will not be a problem. Peer pressure can be a
huge lever for learning; make it work for you by nurturing
an atmosphere where *the students know that the more they support each other's learning, the more they will make outstanding
progress themselves.* When students are speaking or answering,
everyone in the classroom should want to help them make
progress. There must be zero tolerance of mockery and put-
downs and massive compliments for students who can offer
constructive criticism and feedback which is given with love.
This is what I mean by unconditional support; when it
becomes a habit it takes place with or without the teacher in
the classroom.

> 'They are aspirational, know precisely what they need to
> do and are determined to succeed.'
>
> Ofsted (2010)

With the above in place, students will then want to support
you and do well themselves on the day of the inspection.
Enlist their support and be open about what will happen
when an observer speaks to them and asks them about their

learning. Encourage them to be open and honest and answer in detail as much as possible. Be clear about how important they are to this process of judging the lesson and the school. Often teachers say, 'This is not about you being inspected, it's about me. So don't worry.' This is just not true – and they know it. Their books will be checked and they will asked questions and listened to. How they respond will be an important part of the judgement so explain why all this happens and describe how they can talk about their learning and progress.

If any students behave badly, address the behaviour and follow through with any sanctions. Follow the school's behaviour policy (not your own version) rigorously and consistently in all your lessons and do the same when you are observed. If an observer or inspector sees you deal firmly and effectively with any incident you can still get a very positive judgement.

Love your students

It is a basic tenet of neuroscience that learning is an emotional experience. Nothing is more important than you and the aura that you project in the classroom. This includes your relationship with the students and your belief in yourself as a great teacher. As Independent Thinking Associate Dr Andrew Curran says in the introduction to his *The Little Book of Big Stuff about the Brain*: 'The most surprising message for me from looking through billions of dollars of research is that the most important thing you can do for yourself and for others is to love yourself and others for who they are, because by doing that you maximise the brain's ability to learn and unlearn.'

Loving your students can require high quality acting and performing skills! But, as many teachers have discovered, such performances can become a reality. You can learn to love them – even the 'hardcore' students; the ones who seem determined to make you dislike them by challenging your authority and who refuse to participate in learning activities that have taken hours of careful thought and planning. Many of us have surprised ourselves using that tried and tested method of 'pretending' that your least favourite class is, in fact, the class you most enjoy teaching. How do you do this? Simple! Arrive early, instead of as late as possible. Wait with a smile at the door and a personal greeting, especially for the most challenging individuals. Set the highest expectations of behaviour and learning in your opening communications and be consistent in sticking to them in every lesson and with every student.

Great communication and rapport

Communication skills are the most crucial skills that a teacher needs to ensure the best outcomes in lessons – but it is so easy to get it wrong. Rapport exists when you have a connection with your audience which makes their emotional brain feel good and want to be there. You know when you have it when people listen, smile and respond to you.

When you don't have it, you can be as knowledgeable and clever as you like, but no one will be listening.

You get rapport through using an appropriate register. Make it too formal and the students will turn off. Use open, confident body language, good volume and intonation that sounds enthusiastic – even passionate – about your subject. Adapt and tune in to the mood of the classroom. Connect with their world by understanding it. Music, sport, television, computer games, gangs – whatever it takes – make sure you know what will connect with them and try to use it in your teaching. Your job is to create a 'can do' and 'will do' philosophy and to nurture an atmosphere where making mistakes is accepted as an integral part of learning. Be consistent in this. *Every* lesson!

Outstanding spiritual, moral, social and cultural development occurs when 'Pupils think deeply about their own and other's experiences and try to relate them to a clear set of personal values. They have a keen interest in ethical issues, act in a principled manner and understand the importance of reassessing values in the light of experience.'

Ofsted (2010)

Here are some simple examples of good and poor verbal communication.

Good Verbal Communication: What to say

'Good morning! How is my favourite class today?'

'Anything exciting happen at the weekend?'

'I'm really looking forward to teaching you this bit as you're going to love it.'

'I was really impressed with what some of you did for homework. It's some of the best work I've ever seen.'

'Some of you have found it hard but that's good because we are going to learn why, sort it out and get you making great progress.'

'We'll find a way to help you learn this.'

'You are the best class I teach.'

'I love the way you work together so well.'

'You've come up with the most amazing ideas.'

'You've made my day with the work you've produced.'

'I need you to listen and work hard because I know you can do it.'

'When you're at football practice you're so determined. Let's see if you can find some of that motivation and apply it here for me.'

'The way this class supports each other in their learning is outstanding and makes me very proud.'

'Well done for working so hard on that. Tell me what you've learned so far and what else you would like to learn.'

'Brilliant. That work you are doing shows just how hard you're working. What do you need to do to move on to the next level?'

'You're thinking really hard about what you have to do and you'll really make great progress like this.'

'You've redrafted this so many times and that's exactly what you need to do to produce an outstanding piece of writing. Superb effort!'

'You didn't get that right but you kept trying and learned from your mistakes – that makes you a brilliant learner.'

> 'Praise effort more often than outcome.'
>
> Carol Dweck

Poor Verbal Communication: What not to say

'Let's not have another lesson where we waste your time and mine.'

'We have to get through this bit for the exam even though it's hard and boring.'

'I can't believe how many of you just haven't made the effort for homework. You'll never learn anything unless you make more effort.'

'You're really struggling with this so you need to concentrate harder.'

'You're the worst class in Year 8 because you just don't listen.'

'If you don't get on with your work you're wasting my time, so I'll waste your time in break.'

'I don't enjoy this any more than you do.'

'I am so disappointed in the way you are behaving.'

'What would your parents say if they saw the way you are behaving.'

Praising the outcome alone can make students think this is the only result worth achieving and be reluctant to try if they can't get this again:

'Brilliant, 10/10 – a fantastic result. Keep this up.'

'This is A grade work – well done.'

'At last, a C grade – keep this up!'

'Getting there.'

Chapter 3
Assessment *as* learning

AfL [Assessment for Learning] is the process of seeking and interpreting evidence for use by students and their teachers, to decide where the students are in their learning, where they need to go and how best to get there.

Rowe (2007)

Assessment is such an important part of the process of learning, and of making progress in learning, that it deserves a chapter in its own right. The argument put by Dylan Wiliam and Paul Black in *Inside the Black Box* has been won and assessment for learning policy and practice has been driving school improvement strategies because it works (for more information visit http://www.collegenet.co.uk/admin/download/inside%20the%20black%20box_23_doc.pdf).

Assessment *as* learning takes the effective practice of AfL a step further as it recognises that assessment is itself an integral part of the learning process.

An observer will expect your students to know and be able to talk about what level or grade they are at and what they need to do to improve. They will expect to see evidence in the work they have produced of focused marking and targets for improvement. Make sure there is evidence of this in the students' books or notes.

An assessment-centred classroom has been described as follows:

> In assessment-centred classrooms, assessment is both formative and summative and becomes a tool to aid learning: students monitor their progress over time and with their teachers identify the next steps needed to improve. Techniques such as open questioning, sharing learning objectives and focused marking have a powerful effect on students' ability to take an active role in their learning. There is always sufficient time left for reflection by students. Whether individually or in pairs, students are given the opportunity to review what they have learned and how they have learned it. They evaluate themselves and one another in a way that contributes to understanding. Students know their levels of achievement and make progress towards their next goal.
>
> Hargreaves (2005)

This type of teaching clearly encourages independent learning as it gives students the tools for monitoring their own progress. It also links clearly to the Personal, Learning and Thinking skills (PLTs) as it involves the development of reflective learning, self-management and independent enquiry.

Now compare your own practice against the following top tips for 'perfect' assessment *as* learning.

The lesson objectives

1. The objectives must be clear to students. They *all* must know *what* they are learning and *why* they are doing it. They also need to see the point of the objectives in the bigger picture; that is, how they relate to the last lesson's learning, the course they are following and the big overall goal. This means that you can't simply write the objectives on the board and hope that the students merely copy them down. It implies that you have fully explained them in context, the students have engaged with them and can explain them to the observer.

2. The objectives and learning outcomes must be differentiated. All the learners should be able to see where they are and what they need to do to get to the next level. This should link into subject standards and progression where possible. It is crucial to have high expectations of what can be achieved and engage the students with that belief.

3. Success criteria for achieving the outcomes need to be negotiated with the students for optimum engagement to enable them to be clear about what it will look like and feel like and sound like when they have made that progress.

Consider the example below of a learning outcome and differentiated success criteria for an English functional skills lesson. It includes differentiated learning outcomes and shows a visual image of how this represents progress towards a bigger goal which relates to life and other subjects. Students can also mark along this arrow where they think they are at the end of the lesson to show progress (or – just as important – lack of it).

OBJECTIVE: To recognise the power of different types of language

OUTCOMES: I will be able to:

- Use formal and informal language (Entry level).
- Explain how to speak and write in appropriate language (Level 1).
- Teach others how to use a range of writing and speaking styles appropriate for different audiences (Level 2).

Where am I now on the path to the big goal?

| Entry level | | | | Level 1 | | | | Level 2 |

I will be able to use language to be a successful communicator at work and in life.

Chapter 3

Self-assessment

You need to encourage the habit of self-assessment against the learning objectives until it becomes routine. The Assessment of Pupil Progress (APP) criteria for your subject may help with this but they will probably need translating into simple categories as in the table overleaf showing the levels for assessment of reading.

> I have come to the conclusion that my mood and my motivation are a mirror to reflect the mood and motivation of my class.

Level 1	Level 2
✓ I can read aloud words I read a lot. ✓ I can understand what more difficult words mean because I know the alphabet, but I sometimes need help. ✓ I can say why I like some poems and stories.	✓ I can read and understand easy pieces of writing. ✓ I can often work out how to say a word and what it means if I do not know it. ✓ I can say what I think about things which have happened in the story, poem or other writing.

Level 3	Level 4
✓ I can read aloud clearly and without making many mistakes. ✓ I can usually work out what a word means by myself. ✓ I can understand what happens in what I read and can explain what I like and what I do not like. ✓ I can find books in the library, use a dictionary and an index because I know the alphabet.	✓ When I read a story I can say who is in it (the characters) and what happens (the events). ✓ When I read a piece of writing, I can say what it is about (the themes). ✓ I can try to guess what happens in a story and make guesses about why characters do things. ✓ When I talk or write about something I've read I can show someone what I mean in the book. I can find out what I want to know from books.

Note: With thanks to TES Resources.

Level 5	Level 6
✓ I can say what is important about what I have read.	✓ I can see that there may be more than one meaning to texts I have read and I can explain why these are important.
✓ I use examples and quotations from what I have read to show what I mean.	
✓ I can find out what I want to know from books and other sources of information.	✓ I can say what I think about books, poems and plays by looking at the way they are written (the language and the structure) and the themes.
	✓ I can research something I want to know from lots of different sources and write it down.

Level 7	Level 8
✓ I can say how writers use language to say what they want to say. ✓ I can write about themes, structure and the way language is used (linguistic features) in poems, plays and novels. ✓ I can select information from many sources and use it in different ways.	✓ I can write about how an author uses linguistic features, structure and the layout of the text (presentational devices) to influence the reader. ✓ I can select what is relevant in a text and look at how the same information can be presented differently in different types of texts.

Note: With thanks to TES Resources.

Exceptional performance

✓ I can write in detail, develop my ideas and look carefully at the language, structure and presentation of a range of demanding texts.

✓ I can make comparisons between texts including audience, purpose and form.

✓ I can see when information is presented as argument or opinion.

Note: With thanks to TES Resources.

Peer-assessment

Opportunities for peer-assessment are vital in a great lesson. When an observer sees this happening really well in your classroom it will be because you have built up the skills to do it well over time. This, in turn, provides excellent evidence of the quality of your teaching. To nurture great peer-assessment you need to show students how important they are to each other's learning. Use the following five-point plan:

1. Teach students that 'I can learn more by helping others learn', and that when they assess each other's work it improves their own performance. After all, having played the role of assessor they know what is required to impress.

2. Create a culture of unconditional support of each other's learning. Reinforce an atmosphere where the students listen to each other, care about each other making good progress and appreciate constructive criticism.

3. Have zero tolerance of disrespect for the effort of others. This must apply when students are marking each other's work or when they are listening to each other's presentations.

4. Make sure they know and understand the success criteria when assessing each other's work. They can then write targets for each other as they mark each other's work. This will help them to understand how to improve their own work too.

5. Reward high quality peer-assessment as much as you can.

Teacher questioning

More effort has to be spent in framing questions that are worth asking: that is, questions that explore issues that are critical to the development of children's understanding.

Black et al. (2003)

Use open questions that encourage analysis, synthesis and evaluation at critical learning moments to elicit thinking and develop learning. You can do this when students are working on an individual basis or in class discussion.

Work at the top end of Bloom's taxonomy

In the classroom teachers usually concentrate on teaching the lower-order skills in Bloom's taxonomy. However, we need students to use higher-order skills to make learning last. Examples of verbs and question stems, and some activities for each level, are given in the following table.

The following tables further illustrate the top three skills.

Creating

Skill/activity	Verbs	Question stems
Creating Invent a machine to ... Design a ... Write a ... about ...	Imagine. Generalise. Relate. Predict. Conclude. Combine. Modify. Re-arrange. Substitute. Plan. Design. Create. Invent. Compose. Formulate. Prepare. Generalise. Re-write.	Can you design a ... to ... ? Why not compose a song about ... ? Can you see a possible solution to ... ? What would happen if ... ? How many ways can you ... ? Can you create new uses for ...? Can you make a new recipe for ... ? Can you develop a proposal to ...?

Increasing demand ←

Evaluating

Skill/activity	Verbs	Question stems
Evaluating Prepare a case to present your view about ... Convince others that ...	Test. Measure. Rank/grade. Discriminate between. Assess. Verify. Judge. Decide. Select. Choose. Recommend. Convince. Support. Summarise.	Is there a better solution to ... ? Judge the value of ... Can you defend your position about ... ? Is ... a good or a bad thing? How would you have handled ... ? What would you recommend and why? How effective are ... ? What do you think about ... ?

← **Increasing demand**

Analysing

Skill/activity	Verbs	Question stems
Analysing Design a questionnaire to ... Conduct an investigation to ... Construct a graph to show ...	Analyse. Identify. Recognise. See patterns. Select. Order. Organise. Classify. Arrange. Separate. Divide. Explain. Connect. Compare. Contrast. Infer.	How was this similar to ... ? What was the underlying theme of ... ? What are other possible outcomes? Can you explain what happened when ... ? Can you distinguish between ... ? What were the motives behind ... ? What was the problem with ... ?

Source: Bloom (1956)

Increasing demand ◀

These strategies are helpful when implementing successful questioning in the classroom.

Have a no hands-up policy

If no one can put their hand up, they all have to think about the question – especially when you then pick a name from a hat and expect an answer.

Thinking time: pair and share

Set questions they can think about in pairs and get them to come up with several possible answers to share with the rest of the class.

Use connectives to extend thinking

Ask them to use connectives such as 'but', 'therefore', 'however' or 'alternatively' like batons to extend answers. When a student answers, the next one must take over the answer and continue after the connective.

Reflect and review

Use metacognition to reflect on *what* has been learned and *how* it has been learned. As well identifying what supported the learning, reflect on the mistakes made and the obstacles that got in the way (resources, research, friends, trying a different method, etc.).

Ask the students to make up a set of questions about what they have learned and what questions they need to ask for the next stage of their progress. This will require demonstrating an understanding of what they have learned and where they are now.

Assessment for learning in the classroom: what is an observer looking for?

Good (the students do all of this):

- All students know what they are learning and why.
- Students know the success criteria and can self-assess their work against them.
- Students learn openly from each other frequently.
- Students ask reflective questions of their own and other's work.
- Students can constructively criticise each other to support learning.
- All students make good progress with developing independence.

Outstanding (the students do all of the above *plus* all of this):

- Students all understand and can talk about their learning outcomes and set their own individual success criteria.

- Students can use subject terminology as well as a language for learning to discuss and monitor their own progress.

- Students value talking for learning and consciously use it to advance their learning.

- Student questions demonstrate fearless enquiry and a desire to progress.

- Students know exactly where they are, what they have achieved and how to make further progress.

Good (you do all of this):

- Plan and set challenging, differentiated and clear objectives.

- Students are encouraged to set success criteria for the learning outcomes.

- Links are made to other subjects and contexts.

- Grades of progression are known.

- Progress is reviewed with students regularly throughout the lesson.

- The teacher uses skilful questioning and resources to encourage sustained successful collaborative work.

- The teaching is flexible and responds to learning needs – adjusting whenever appropriate to make maximum progress.

- Marking is focused and sets clear targets that relate to learning needs and engages students so they take action.

Outstanding
(you do all of the above *plus* all of this):

- The teacher sets big goals and has very high expectations of all students in the lesson and over time.
- Progression in the Personal, Learning and Thinking skills (PLTs) and subject concepts is integral to the planning of the lesson.
- The teacher is constantly coaching students in understanding how their learning is progressing and how to recognise it.
- Class discussion is skilfully developed to nurture thinking and encourage independence.
- The teacher and the students develop the learning together in response to the advancement made.
- The teacher plans next steps with students in response to the progress made in the lesson.
- There is clear evidence that marking impacts on students by helping them to make exceptional progress.

Chapter 4

Independent learning in the classroom

Who works hardest in your classroom – you or the students? In your lessons are your students willing to ask questions, take decisions, select appropriate resources independently and learn from mistakes - or are they dependent on you?

To develop the habits of independent learning amongst your students takes time and skill but is rewarded in the long run. You will be less exhausted, your students will be more empowered and successful – and your lesson evaluations will be graded outstanding!

> 'The quality of learning is exceptional. Pupils demonstrate excellent concentration and are rarely off task, even for extended periods without direction from an adult. They have developed resilience when tackling challenging activities. Their keenness and commitment to succeed in all aspects of school life and ability to grasp opportunities to extend and improve their learning are exceptional.'   Ofsted (2010)

This description of 'outstanding' learning shows the importance of demonstrating in lessons that students are fully and personally engaged in the work that they are doing. Students are not driven by the teacher directing the activities or controlling the outcomes. Nor are they reliant on the teacher to provide the motivation through carrot or stick. Ideally, students must be self-motivated, resilient and driven to make progress in their own learning.

How do we achieve this in classrooms built on the didactic principle that the teacher knows best and knows all? In these classrooms, the teacher has control of the key that unlocks the secret knowledge required for exam success. And teachers do have this key: the expertise built from years of accumulated knowledge and the experience of techniques that work to enable their students to pass exams. Teachers enjoy the power that this gives them when students want to learn. There is no better feeling than having a class hanging on to your every word as you 'stage the reveal' in a poem or scientific theory or show the quick way to remember a formula in maths.

However, the role of the teacher when it comes to developing independence in the learner is that of a knowledgeable, highly skilled mentor who is passionate about giving students the skills to find out *for themselves*. This is disparaged by some as child-centred, time-wasting nonsense that distracts from the important job of transferring information from the wise, learned head of the teacher into the empty, eager young mind of the student, through listening and writing from books and the board; a process whose validity is then supported by success in the narrow confines of a written test or exam. But the neuroscience of learning shows that this type of learning is superficial and quickly evaporates. Finding out information for themselves and then presenting, performing and teaching it to each other is a far more powerful way of creating learning that lasts.

'Finding new ways to nurture independent and creative thinkers is a key part of preparing children for life, work and play in today's changing society.'

Steve Beswick, Director of Education, Microsoft UK.

John Crossland worked with advanced skills teachers (ASTs) to discover how brain-based research could be used to help improve learning in the classroom. He found that these ASTs were 'convinced that their already outstanding practice had significantly improved' through using Cognitive Acceleration through Science Education (CASE) thinking skills packages, which encourage collaborative, reflective learning based around the underlying principle that all learning has an emotional component.

However, even these excellent teachers still found it hard to let go of the control that the didactic model of teaching promotes: 'They often struggled to implement the counter-intuitive technique of standing back from intervening (non-intervention) in the learning processes during pupil collaborative group work and encouraging pupil metacognition (thinking about thinking) during the review/plenary' (Crossland 2010).

Teachers don't like to feel superfluous to requirements and often have such a strong work ethic that they feel a compulsion to be in control and want to be needed for their expert input. This is why even ASTs needed help to let go of the didactic model and encourage more independent learning habits in their students. However, many teachers (particularly those teaching vocational subjects) are already very good at this facilitation model of pedagogy. Some individuals find it a challenge not to be the 'sage on the stage' as opposed to 'the guide from the side', but most teachers can expand their professional ability in this area and enjoy the rewards of seeing students 'turning their own light bulbs on' by developing for themselves the required learning skills.

Chapter 4

How to develop independent learning in the classroom

To start, raise awareness of and then teach the learning skills, using the Personal, Learning and Thinking skills (PLTs) as a framework. Students can be taught to focus on exactly what the skills of an 'independent enquirer' are and on how well they are applying them.

The PLTs have evolved from the 'learning to learn' theory and are identified as the skills required by employers:

Independent enquirers
Young people who process and evaluate information in their investigations, planning what to do and how to go about it. They take informed and well-reasoned decisions, recognising that others have different beliefs and attitudes.

Creative thinkers
Young people who think creatively by generating and exploring ideas and making original connections. They try different ways to tackle a problem, working with others to find imaginative solutions and outcomes that are of value.

Reflective learners
Young people who evaluate their strengths and limitations as learners and set themselves realistic goals and

criteria for success. They monitor their own performance and progress, inviting feedback from others and making changes to improve their learning.

Teamworkers
Young people who work confidently with others, adapting to different contexts and taking responsibility for their own role. They listen and take account of other's views. They form collaborative relationships, resolving issues to reach agreed outcomes.

Self-managers
Young people who organise themselves, showing personal responsibility, initiative, creativity and enterprise with a commitment to learning and self-improvement. They actively embrace change, responding positively to new priorities, coping with challenges and looking for opportunities.

Effective participators
Young people who actively engage with issues that affect them and those around them. They play a full part in the life of their school, college, workplace or wider community by taking responsible action to bring improvements for others as well as themselves.

It is important to develop all of the PLTs in the classroom – but good, independent learners need first to become good, independent enquirers.

Good independent enquirers have the following skills. They:

- Identify clearly the questions to answer and problems to sort out.
- Plan and carry out research and understand how choices affect outcome.
- Explore issues and events or problems from different points of view.
- Analyse information and judge how important it is.
- Understand how decisions and events can be affected by the situation, people's beliefs and feelings.
- Back up their conclusions using thoughtful arguments and reasoning.

The table overleaf gives a good starting point for students to consider how well-developed their independent enquiry skills are:

Logging the development of independent enquiry skills	Activities to develop the skills	Links to other PLTs/subjects
I identify questions to answer and problems to sort out Never Sometimes Usually Always →	Survival challenge on a desert island Plan a holiday Organise a charity fundraising event Five whys	*Teamworker* Science RS Citizenship PSHE
I plan and carry out research and understand how choices affect outcome Never Sometimes Usually Always →	Use search engines to research a topic in groups. Use different key words then compare the results Undertake a survey to assess student attitudes using different questions Compare the impact of questions on results	*Reflective learner* ICT English

Logging the development of independent enquiry skills	Activities to develop the skills	Links to other PLTs/subjects
I explore issues and events or problems from different points of view Never Sometimes Usually Always	Take a current national, local or school subject issue: ▪ PMI (Plus, Minus, Interesting) bits ▪ Six Thinking Hats ▪ Eight Way Thinking Tool Role play edition of *Question Time* or the *Jeremy Kyle Show*	*Effective participator* Citizenship RS
I analyse information and judge how important it is Never Sometimes Usually Always	Examine several sources and place them in order of importance (e.g. newspaper article, encyclopaedia entry, horoscope, government White Paper statements, novel extract, graph, road sign)	*Reflective learner* Science History English

Logging the development of independent enquiry skills	Activities to develop the skills	Links to other PLTs/subjects
I understand how decisions and events can be affected by the situation, people's beliefs and feelings Never Sometimes Usually Always →	Collect images and film clips with an emotive quality In groups discuss what is happening, why and what will happen next Evaluate and feedback how these answers were reached	*Creative thinker* Media/Art English
I back up my conclusions using thoughtful arguments and reasons Never Sometimes Usually Always →	Use connectives to draw out detailed responses. Hold up a card with one of these on whenever a student thinks they have finished summing up a conclusion (e.g. but, also, because, however, alternatively, nevertheless, although, unless, except, for example, whereas, or)	*Self-manager* English History

Once students have become aware of the skills required for independent learning – and of the need to continually develop them and how they link to all subjects – then the scene is set to enable the students to demonstrate the independent learning described earlier by Ofsted. The long-term outcome will be to develop in our students the deep, sustainable learning habits that will also, believe it or not, ensure success in exams.

> 'Students need the attitudes and skills of independence for long term success … Ironically, independence that is built into many primary schools during Key Stages 1 and 2 is dismantled in many secondary schools during Key Stage 3, only to be required again at Key Stage 4 [and even more so at Key Stage 5!].'
>
> Ginnis (2002)

Seven steps to independent learning

1. **Set big long-term goals** which will influence the learning outcomes of each lesson. We always underestimate what our students can do and a crucial measure of your success will be *how high your expectations are*. Give the students the bigger picture of how their lives can be altered for the better. Go beyond the classroom, school and exams towards life and personal success in order to engage the emotional brain.

2. **Have clear required learning outcomes *and* skills to be developed** planned into individual lessons. Around 70 per cent of the lesson must be *collaborative work and active learning*. This means students talking with each other and doing. Build in maximum *choice* of activity to facilitate self-differentiation. Allow *flexibility* as the nature of these lessons means that the students may work faster or differently to expectation, and your job is to adjust the framework for maximum progress. Build in a *surprise* such as an additional resource or change of brief to encourage resilience. Plan *reflective strategies* that encourage self-assessment of the learning at several stages and at the end of the lesson.

3. **Set the emotional environment for learning** by delivering your input with passion and enthusiasm. It has to matter to you in order to engage the emotional brains of your students. Ensure that the groups are skilled in understanding how important good teamwork is through preparation and coaching in team roles and dynamics. Especially important is a feeling of safety and support amongst the group for the whole team. This can be enhanced over time by rewarding good leadership and inclusive behaviours.

4. **Include challenge and competition** to enhance the team-building process. Setting teams to compete against each other for points or throwing in additional unexpected challenges all help to unite them and focus their activity.

5. **Plan your interventions into their group work.** Allow the students themselves, as far as possible, to work through the problems they may have with the task and with group relationships. If you do need to intervene or help, limit the number of questions they can ask you by issuing question cards. Ensure that these questions promote metacognition (thinking about thinking). Encourage the students to find out answers for themselves. Always answer a question with a question. Discuss a solution with one team member and get him or her to teach it to the rest of the group.

6. **Use assessment *as* learning.** When students complete the tasks assigned they should each:

   ▨ critically appraise the work they have completed;

   ▨ discuss their role in the outcome;

   ▨ say how well they have met the objectives;

   ▨ and, crucially, say what *progress* they have made.

The notes the students make will inform the quality control aspect of the learning outcome. A simple way for students to remember this is that they will need AIMS (Amend, Improve, Measure and Share (peer-assess)). They will need to do this several times during a project before they can become proficient at assessing and demonstrating their learning.

7. **Review and reflection.** When students have been working outside your supervision in a lesson this is your chance to monitor how much they have achieved.

They can log their skills in independent learning using the first column in the tables above (pp. 76-78). How much of this did they do and can they tell you when and where? Can they demonstrate the skill they have acquired or the learning progress they have made? Can they say to each other, on a sticky note or in class discussion, *how* they learned it, motivated themselves, solved problems, worked with others and so on?

This important reflection is in addition to the mini-plenaries or assessment for learning strategies. It is a planned period of metacognition about the whole activity or project that links learning to home, big goals and other subjects. This could entail keeping a learning log or making a presentation to the class about how the learning worked and how their skills in independent learning are developing. Such a performance will enhance their recognition of progress and develop their language for learning. This reflective practice will help them learn from their mistakes and have a critical appreciation of their work, as well as an understanding of what motivates them.

It can take a lifetime to understand how to make the best of our own amazing learning preferences and potential – most of that lifetime journey takes place once we have left school. Why does work teach us so much more about the best way to learn?

Embedding learning skills for life

By using the previous strategies consistently across the curriculum and over time, the students will develop their interpersonal skills, confidence, self-reliance, risk taking and the ability to challenge their own and other's thinking. These are skills which students use without thinking when mastering a new mobile phone, computer game, downloading music, using Facebook or learning a new dance.

The teacher's role is to highlight the *process* of learning in their classrooms and develop a language which describes that process. Teachers must also give students opportunities to own the process for themselves and to reflect on their learning.

Independent learning in the classroom, in essence, simply taps into, further reinforces and makes explicit the pre-existing skills and motivation within our students. If we can provide the right stimuli and encourage their commitment to succeed, we will ensure that our students develop real, deep, lasting learning and a set of life skills which will more effectively equip them for the real world. And, oh yes, exam grades will improve too!

'Success in exams is still considered important but is increasingly viewed as the secondary result of excellent learning.'

2010 presentation by Ofsted Inspector Rob Hubbleday (citing Ofsted 2009)

Chapter 5

Making teamwork work: productive collaborative learning

This chapter focuses on how to ensure that the collaborative work you do with students when being observed is hooked quite firmly into the *progress* in learning that we want to achieve. For many fabulous examples and ideas for group work activity see *The Teacher's Toolkit* by Paul Ginnis.

Use the Personal, Learning and Thinking skills (PLTs) model to ensure that students become aware of the importance of the *explicit* development of thinking skills, subject expertise, subject skills, effective participation in learning conversations, reflective learning and self-managing. These are the employability skills that will create the flexible learners we need in the twenty-first century. Plan your collaborative projects to develop each of the PLTs then use the model in group work to assess how well they have developed the relevant skills.

Chapter 5

What does Ofsted look for?

The questions below are from the guidance for inspectors on evaluating teaching (the quality of learning):

Inspectors may well focus on questions such as these when observing lessons:

- What are the students actually learning as opposed to doing?
- Are they learning something new?
- Can all students make links between previous and new learning?
- Can the students talk about what they are learning or simply describe what they are doing?
- Do they produce work of a consistently good standard?
- Are they working independently? Are they self-reliant?
- How well do they collaborate?
- Do they show initiative?

Ensuring that *all* your students are making progress when they are working in groups is a key part of your planning and your intervention. This chapter aims to ensure that group work in your lessons demonstrates optimal collaboration for learning.

Remember: more group work means more active learning by the students and less talking by you.

> 'Students should have three times as much time doing stuff in lessons than you spend chatting at them.'
>
> Beadle (2010)

How to form groups

Young people like to work with their friends and sometimes this works well, but on occasions it reinforces prejudices towards others and is too easy. Vary the groups so that students are challenged to work with a variety of different people and become conscious of the need to negotiate, mediate and facilitate each other's learning. Explain that working with a range of individuals may feel uncomfortable but this will make them more flexible and better communicators. Reinforce the 'unconditional support' ethos from Chapter 2 so that they strive to engage everyone in the group and ensure all are progressing.

> 'Whatever the activity or learning a class led discussion will never be as engaging as brilliantly engineered small group discussion ... It is in the setting of paired or grouped discussion work that you can mark yourself out as the kind of teacher who has thought properly about how learning works, and who is in possession of a special level of super-cool, advanced pedagogical skills.'
>
> Beadle (2010)

> 'The campaign for self-discipline and collective responsibility is well worth the effort.'
>
> Ginnis (2002)

For maximum flexibility and to extend teamworking skills, vary the groupings by using:

- Ability groups and sometimes mixed ability groups.
- Gender groups.
- PLTs groups (i.e. put all the skilled creative thinkers in one group or all the good teamworkers in another).
- Expert groups. If some students know more about the subject, group them together for a discussion then disseminate them across the other groups later.
- Friendship groups. Total choice or friendship pairs merged together.
- Random groups. Pull names out of a hat to surprise them.

For each group session make sure the students fill in a simple group- and self-assessment sheet that focuses on learning progress. For example:

How did our group do?	How did I do?
What did we learn? Even better if we ...	What did I learn? Even better if I ...

Group dynamics

In the perfect lesson, the purpose and point of teamwork is to enhance the learning progress of *all* members of the group. It is important to tell students that it is normal for groups to go through challenges and disagreements and that this is when they learn how to improve their teamwork skills. Remember to teach the four stages of good group formation described on page 23 (forming, storming, norming and performing), so that both students and teachers accept the need for teams to resolve problems themselves. Accept that storming will happen and fall-outs will occur but that the students have to resolve this – and doing so will improve their communication skills and empathy. Teach how sports teams, quiz teams or army battalions succeed most when they work together. This will help to give an insight into the synergy that can be created in collaborative learning.

For an 'outstanding' Ofsted evaluation, students are 'highly considerate and very supportive of each other in lessons' (Ofsted 2010).

An example of outstanding learning and teaching: BTEC Sport Year 10: soft tissue injuries (25 students)

- Lively, fun, active session referenced to clear lesson objectives.
- Very encouraging and supportive ethos.
- Genuine collaboration within groups.
- Gifted and Talented students assessing and coaching others.
- Lesson builds well on previous learning with good understanding of technical terms allowing in-depth discussion of techniques.
- Teacher monitors understanding and development: listens, questions, explains, summarises.
- All students fully involved and making excellent progress.

Make the main aim of group work to enhance the learning and performance of each other. Imagine that your life depended on *all* of you doing well!

A culture of collaborative learning will help everyone accept the central goal (or norm) of the group: *We all need to make this work so that we can all learn as much as possible.* Quite often students get caught up in the drive towards the outcome rather than realising the power of the process.

If the main aim of the team is to produce the very best water rocket (see the collaborative activity on pages 26-27) then some of the group may dominate and take over. However, if you want *all* students to make progress then the group needs to be aware that everyone must know what is going on and contribute to making the rocket work. The team must be very clear about the outcomes required. For example, it could be 'the best rocket made by the best teamwork'; so a high quality outcome produced by just one member of the group would not be acceptable. This must be acknowledged in the success criteria.

Groups must have a set of rules that make it second nature to behave in certain ways as they work together. For example:

- We will all take turns to speak.
- We will all get the chance to speak.
- We will listen to each other when we speak.
- We will support each other's contributions and collectively prevent any negative comments.
- We will all help each other to learn as much as possible from this activity.
- We will all work hard to make our team successful.

What follows is an example of notes taken by an observer in a Year 9 science lesson where outstanding learning and teaching was seen in practical group work:

STUDENTS: Actively engaged in answering questions; peer review of their answers leads to well-focused discussion; students confident to query what the teacher has said; excellent planning and practical work in groups; all groups are working hard and making significant progress in understanding.

TEACHER: Enforces time limits; reviews early answers; targets questions well; circulates between groups and discusses understanding; organises smooth transition from planning to activity; stops lesson to highlight learning.

Teaching each other is the most powerful way for young people to learn.

Group roles

Encouraging groups to allocate different responsibilities to different students will help the group work well and give the students a chance to reflect on how well they fulfilled the role. Roles within team could include some or all of the following:

- Motivator
- Coach
- Scribe
- Clerk
- Leader
- Chairperson
- Finisher
- Completer
- Ideas generator
- Challenger
- Expert

Students can also both *evolve* and *revolve* – evolve roles for the group according to the task and activity and be encouraged to revolve the different responsibilities so they can practise various skills and develop flexibility. When teamwork is good, and this becomes routine, then students will be able to talk to an observer about their role, their learning within the group and how well it worked on this occasion and at other times in the past.

Chapter 5

Leadership: the optimum skill for teacher and student

Leadership is about taking responsibility and being accountable for the outcomes. All students should have an opportunity to take the lead role on various occasions. Rewarding leaders for managing their team effectively so that *everyone* achieves a good learning outcome will be an important part of your lesson. Teach students about leadership and model effective teaching as leadership in the classroom.

Leadership can take various forms:

- *Quiet leadership* that leads from the background but gives the team confidence.
- *Inspiring leadership* that sets an example through hard work and taking risks.
- *Democratic leadership* that makes sure everyone has their say and feels part of the decisions made.
- *Determined leadership* that never gives up and ensures the job is done.

In the plenary for the lesson help students to consider:

- How did the leadership work in our group?
- What difference did it make to the outcome?
- How could it be better?

The question asked at the end of the BBC's *Apprentice* is always: Was he or she a good leader? Good leaders don't get fired!

How do you know they are learning?

Mastering the management of really good collaborative learning is very challenging because the teacher must know how the team activity is progressing the learning for *all* students. You may need to intervene in the group work at key moments to consolidate the learning and demonstrate the progress. You can use a progress arrow or the Assessment of Pupil Progress (APP) progression model to aid the metacognition process by asking how far they have moved towards the learning outcome.

For example:

No idea	Some	Most	Got it!	I can explain the difference between solids and gases physically and at a molecular level.
	But I can explain what I do/do not get.		Ask me anything.	

The best way of measuring progress is to build some proper DIRT (Dedicated Improvement and Reflection Time) into the plenary at the end of all collaborative work.

Regularly reviewing what has been learned and how it has happened using the arrow method or any of the other methods described is the key to developing a routine and habit where students discuss and measure their own individual progress towards your tightly set differentiated objectives.

In this way your lesson is rigorous, adds value and (hopefully) demonstrates outstanding progress.

At the end of the lesson, the test of great collaborative learning will be for students to ask themselves:

- What did I learn in this lesson?
- How did my group help or hinder my learning?
- How much progress have I made in my subject's skills and knowledge?
- How much progress have I made with my teamworking skills?

You should consider how aware you are of the progress being made by all groups of students, particularly the progress of those with specific needs (the most able, the special education needs child, the quiet boy, the disruptive girl, etc.). To ensure they are making progress will require well-crafted support to make for 'perfect' collaborative learning.

Now you just have to plan the next lesson …

Chapter 6

Top tips for using human and other resources effectively to enhance progress in learning

'Resources, including new technology, make a marked contribution to the quality of learning, as does the precisely targeted support provided by other adults ... Teachers and other adults are acutely aware of their pupils' capabilities and of their prior learning and understanding, and plan very effectively to build on these ... Marking and dialogue between teachers, other adults and pupils are consistently of a very high quality ... Pupils understand in detail how to improve their work and are consistently supported in doing so.'

Ofsted (2010)

The use of all the resources available to you to make the learning work is an important part of the perfect lesson. This is a huge area and this chapter provides just a selection of examples of good practice that may be helpful in ensuring you create a great lesson.

> Ask yourself: If you plan to use ICT or have learning support assistants or teaching assistants in your lesson, how will they make a difference to the learning?

What follows are a few top tips for using teaching assistants (TAs) or any other adult in your classroom. For further information and expert advice see Phil Beadle's *How to Teach* and Jim Smith's *The Lazy Teacher's Handbook*.

- Ensure they have a copy of the lesson plan and make sure they are mentioned in it!
- Try to discuss it in advance with them and plan for them to take an active role.
- The active role can be within a group activity that may be enhanced by the presence of an adult. If you do this make certain the TA is fully briefed about how to facilitate a group activity without taking it over.
- A section of the lesson can be delivered by the TA. This is particularly successful when they are confident and can include some of their own expertise or experience. For example, in a science lesson they could describe the impact of a wind farm near their home or in a maths lesson discuss the way they use functional maths skills at home. Often the TA will have knowledge from personal

interests or study. Make sure you know about these and use them. Students love it when you vary the input.

- Use the TA to observe and record skills development with a small number of students for assessment purposes. This is especially useful when groups are working together and you want to know how particular students with certain needs are performing in the group dialogue or activity. This can be followed up by an individual discussion with the student concerned as a support to the DIRT (Dedicated Improvement and Reflection Time).

- Use TAs to support students who have problems with English as a second language but remember to plan this in advance so that the TA has a list of the key words translated and you have agreed upon scaffolded tasks.

- If TAs are working with particular students, make sure they are not doing the work for them and ask them to report to you about the progress made by that student and the next steps that are needed.

Chapter 6

Using ICT

Technology is such an integral part of the learning that it is sure to be built into your long-term schemes and plans. However it must be subject to the question: *How is it contributing to the progress in learning of the students?* Some of the best cross-curricular uses of ICT are listed below:

- Interactive (for) games and quizzes that rehearse mental arithmetic or vocabulary.
- Student participation by voting for answers.
- Laptops for researching historical events.
- Showing films and clips as examples of narrative development.
- Students filming themselves to see skills development in PE and reflect on progress and next steps.
- Mobile phone text messages, emails, tweets and blogs used as a learning review to engage students in sharing what they have learned.
- Presenting learning to others.

Other resources

Interesting resources can make a lesson engaging and impress any observer. Novelty engages the emotional brain – which explains why students always remember the lesson when you wore the horned helmet to discuss the Vikings. However, the resources must always contribute to, not distract from, the progress the students are making in learning.

In his useful checklist for what constitutes an outstanding lesson, Tim Hann (2010) when describing use of resources said: 'Periods of teacher-led information are short. They use ingenious techniques and innovative aids and resources, directly facilitating student curiosity, query, engagement, and a desire to tackle the learning'

Tony Thornley (2007) in his article stated, 'The teaching is exciting and interesting (for example, through use of stimulating resources or other adults in the lesson); it may be inspired, although it doesn't have to be.' Also, 'Students have easy access to, and make use of, additional resources which they use independently to support or enhance their learning.'

Some examples of resources that have worked well in lessons include:

- Powerful images, still or moving.
- Artefacts that are mysterious (like a closed box with something magic inside) or shocking (such as a real brain or lungs).
- Wigs or masks worn by the teacher or students.
- Toys such as soft balls, models, puppets and so on will grab the interest of the class no matter what their age. If they can contribute to the learning then they will certainly provide engaging activities.
- A real live expert on the subject – someone from the community who can tell a relevant story, a business expert or an ex-pupil will be a very impressive addition to your 'perfect' lesson.

Finally, a word of warning: wonderful resources are exciting and engaging but when planning your perfect lesson always remember to ask:

How much do the resources contribute to the progress the students are making in learning?

Don't get distracted!

The Perfect Ofsted Lesson
Quick checklist

Have you:

1. Set a learning objective that you can measure progress against for different groups of students? ☑

2. Included a subject or personal skills objective within it or separate to it? ☑

3. Planned a lesson with a high proportion of active, independent learning and collaborative activity? ☑

4. Built assessment *as* learning into your lesson? ☑

5. Identified various groups of students in your class and any special needs? ☑

6. Ensured your students have been taught how to work well together and give unconditional support for each other's learning? ☑

7. Built a way to address those needs in your lesson to ensure differentiation? ☑

8. Made sure students are really challenged in the activities and through the reflection? ☑

9. Planned with any TA how they are going to contribute to student progress? ☑

10. Mentally rehearsed it going brilliantly? ☑

Good luck!

Postscript

And afterwards ...
feedback is the breakfast of champions

Ofsted inspections from 2010 involve a higher number of lesson observations as part of the process of evaluating school performance. This means that is it much more likely than ever that you will be observed. It is also possible that you will be observed by two people – one of whom will be from your senior leadership team. When it is over, remember that all teachers observed for more than 20 minutes are entitled to feedback.

Get that feedback, write it down and learn from it. Ask questions and be sure you know what *you* have learned from the experience and how to improve next time. Note down quotes so that you can remember exactly what was said. If you disagree with the judgements say why and ask for clear development points to work on. There is more emphasis than ever on the observation leading to support and improvement and it not being an outcome in itself. If a member of your leadership team was present request further feedback from them later. Remember ...

There is no such thing as failure – only feedback.

If you learn from the experience, lesson observations will be a very constructive part of your progression towards outstanding teaching. *All* teachers have had bad experiences in lesson observations. As was said in the introduction – *Most of the very best teachers have experienced an unsatisfactory judgement at some time in their careers. Learn from it, and it will work as a positive force in your development. Dwell on it, beat yourself up about it, argue about it and it could be destructive and very demoralising.*

Remember, an observation is only a brief snapshot of your teaching. It could turn out to be a wonderful portrait or it could be an unflattering passport photo from one of those booths! Either way it is just a snapshot. The aim of this book is to make that brief observation not only look outstanding but for it to truly reflect your everyday outstanding teaching.

Lots of teachers can put on a flattering, made-up pose – but it is difficult, if not impossible, for even the best of them to magic outstanding lessons out of nowhere with only two days notice.

Following the advice in this book takes time, but if you can implement at least some of it in your day-to-day teaching, that outstanding grade is within your reach.

References and further reading

Beadle, P. (2010). *How To Teach*. Carmarthen: Crown House Publishing.

Beere, J. and Boyle, H. (2009). *The Competency Curriculum Toolkit: Developing the PLTS Framework through Themed Learning.* Carmarthen: Crown House Publishing.

Black, P., Harrison, C., Lee, C., Marshall, B. and Wiliam, D. (2003). *Assessment for Learning: Putting it into Practice.* Buckingham: Open University Press.

Bloom, B. S. (1956). Taxonomy of Educational Objectives, Handbook I: *The Cognitive Domain.* New York: David McKay Co. Inc.

Crossland, J. (2010). Brain biology and learning. *School Science Review*, 337: 99–108.

Curran, A. (2008). *The Little Book of Big Stuff about the Brain.* Carmarthen: Crown House Publishing.

Farr, S. and Teach for America (2010). *Teaching as Leadership: The Highly Effective Teacher's Guide to Closing the Achievement Gap.* San Francisco: Jossey-Bass.

Gilbert, I. (2007). *The Little Book of Thunks*. Carmarthen: Crown House Publishing.

Gilbert, I. (2008). *The Book of Thunks*. Carmarthen: Crown House Publishing.

Ginnis, P. (2002). *The Teacher's Toolkit*. Carmarthen: Crown House Publishing.

Hann, T. (2010). You've Been Framed. *Leader* (published by the Association of School and College Leaders), issue no. 50. Available from http://archive.leadermagazine.co.uk.

Hargreaves, D. (chair) (2005). *About Learning: Report of the Learning Working Group*. London: Demos. Available from http://www.demos.co.uk/files/About_learning. pdf?1240939425.

Jackson, N. (2009). *The Little Book of Music for the Classroom: Using Music to Improve Memory, Motivation, Learning and Creativity*. Carmarthen: Crown House Publishing.

Ofsted (2009). Twelve outstanding secondary schools: Excelling against the odds. Ref. no. 080240. Available from http://www.ofsted.gov.uk/Ofsted-home/Publications-and-research/Browse-all-by/Documents-by-type/Thematic-reports/Twelve-outstanding-secondary-schools-Excelling-against-the-odds/%28language%29/eng-GB.

Ofsted (2010). Evaluation schedule of judgements for schools inspected under section five of the Education Act 2005, from September 2009. Ref. no: 090098. Available from http://

References

www.ofsted.gov.uk/Ofsted-home/Forms-and-guidance/
Browse-all-by/Other/General/Evaluation-schedule-of-
judgements-for-schools-inspected-under-section-five-of-the-
Education-Act-2005-from-September-2009.

Rowe, J. (2007). My top ten tips: Assessment for learning.
Secondary Teachers Magazine, July 2007. Available from http://
www.teachernet.gov.uk/teachers/issue51/secondary/features/
Mytop10tipsAssessmentforLearning.

Smith, J. (2010). *The Lazy Teacher's Handbook: How Your
Students Learn More When You Teach Less*. Carmarthen: Crown
House Publishing.

Thornley, T. (2007). Make it Outstanding. *Leader* (published
by the Association of School and College Leaders), issue no.
19. Available from http://archive.leadermagazine.co.uk.

Tuckman, B. (1965). Developmental sequence in small
groups. *Psychological Bulletin*, 63(6): 384–399.

Wiliam, D. and Black, P. (2006). *Inside the Black Box: Raising
Standards through Classroom Assessment*. London: NFER Nelson.

More Little Books ...